STINKY SHORTS

by

Rex Bell

A collection of short essays inspired by my old buddy Stinky Wilmont, who along with my Mom and Dad, taught me just about everything I really needed to know about life and libertarianism.

Dedicated to my wife Susan,

who I probably ignored even more

than usual while I was putting this

together, and who offered

encouragement,

even when I wasn't listening.

Preface

When I was in the 5th grade, I wrote a poem for an English assignment, and the teacher sent it in to the Hagerstown Exponent, a local weekly paper at the time. As I recall, it was far from a literary masterpiece, but I certainly did enjoy writing it.

I still enjoy writing. This is a compilation of things I've worked on over the last few years. You'll probably notice a theme leaning towards personal freedom, personal responsibility, and limited government. Probably because I think those things are important for the future of our families and our country.

A lot of the stories in this book have numbers pertaining to government spending and debt. I left some space above and below those stories so you can write in new numbers as the situation changes.

Hopefully we can make those numbers smaller.

Contents

Millville Grade School

That's Really Sorry.. 1

We Just Can't Take It... 5

Out On A Limb 9

Stinky and the Secret Spy Ring 13

Swap Meat..16

Harold the Frog..19

Uncle Pug...23

Rights vs. Abilities 26

Relatively Speaking 29

That's Not Really What I had Planned 33

Tipping Points 36

Different Strokes..39

When We Got a Little Older

Stinky's First Car..45

Tolerable Differences 48

Guess Again 52

Wanna Bet 56

Ugly Cars and Pretty Women...............................60

Can You Dig It 64

Merry Christmas and Happy New Year

I'm Sorry, Did You Say Something?........................71

You Say You Want a Resolution.............................75

A Long Weight 78

Christmas Cards and Credit Cards 82

Promises and Resolutions.....................................86

Sorry Virginia 89

Decisions, Decisions, Decisions............................92

More Thoughts on Less Government

Great Expectations 97

Summit, Stinky, and Sisyphus 101

Banjo and Stinky 105

Keep It Simple 109

Finding Our Way 113

Pay 'Em Now, and Pay 'Em Later 117

Pinned Down 122

Whatcha Gonna Do 126

Promises and Pensions 130

A Little More on Libertarianism and Libertarians

Libertarianism 101...My Version..............137

How I Got Here 141

Stinky and Me

and

Millville Grade School

That's Really Sorry

Back at Millville Grade School, Summit Taylor's furnace room also doubled as the teachers' smoking lounge. Nothing fancy, mind you, but it did have a couple of vinyl covered chairs and one of those ashtrays on a stand, with a button that you pushed to send the ashes and crushed butts down to the base of the stand. I think Summit dumped it in the coal furnace when it got full and you couldn't push the button anymore. They probably wouldn't let him do that nowadays.

Whenever we were out for recess, and Summit was out taking care of his janitorial duties, and the teachers weren't smoking in the furnace room, my old buddy Stinky Wilmont would occasionally sneak in and swipe a cigarette or two. I don't know if he really liked to smoke them, or if he just liked the way he looked when he stuck one of them behind his ear. Maybe he just wanted to prove he could get away with it.

Whatever his reasoning, he never seemed to think there was really anything wrong with stealing, or smoking, or sticking cigarettes behind his ear. At least until Principal Walters caught him in the furnace room with a couple of the principal's smokes. When the wood and smoke cleared, the tearful Stinky was a changed man, and quite remorseful about his despicable actions.

I guess it's possible that he had seen the error of his ways, but his revelation would have carried a little more weight if it had occurred after he had swiped only a couple of cigarettes, instead of waiting to appear after he was caught.

There's something that's called a moral compass. Most people have one, I think. Not everybody's points in the same direction, for sure, but I do appreciate people with firm convictions, even if our compasses don't always line up. At least I know which way it's pointing.

Mark Sanford, the South Carolina Governor who had at least a two year long affair with his mistress from Argentina, had a revelation similar to Stinky's when he was caught, metaphorically speaking, with his pants down. I understand that we are all subject to temporary lapses in judgment, but Mr. Sanford's remorseful tone would have been a little more convincing if he had adopted it a year and a half or so before he got caught.

I felt the same way when I heard Bernie Madoff, the con man who bilked investors out of billions of dollars, explain how horrible he felt about what he had done. If he was actually sorry for his actions, and not just about getting caught, I would have thought his conscience would have kicked in a few billion dollars earlier.

I realize the world is way too big to expect everyone to agree on what is moral or ethical. But I do think if our sense of right or wrong is based on what we think we can get away with, or if it's based on the fear of punishment from our principal, or our spouse, or our government, or if it changes only after we're caught, we might want to consider getting our compass recalibrated.

Millville Grade School, where Stinky and I got our learnin'.

We just can't take it...

50 some odd years ago my mother brought a couple boxes of cereal home from the Becker Brothers grocery store in New Castle. I can't for the life of me remember what type or brand of cereal it was, but I vividly remember the prize that was in each box. It was an authentic Rin Tin Tin ballpoint pen, shaped like a genuine repeating rifle that was used by Rinty's cavalry troop and Corporal Carson. My older brother and I nearly foundered on that cereal trying to eat our way to those ink pens, and our diligence finally paid off. In a matter of days, we were each the proud owner of one of the pens.

My brother put his pen in his desk, but I was anxious to show my good fortune off to my pals at Millville Grade School. And, as was often the case so many times in those days, my brother still had his ink pen, while mine was missing, either out on the playground, or behind one of the registers in Mrs. Dilling's room, or under one of the seats on Howard Tucker's bus, or in that no account Stinky Wilmont's lunch bucket.

Regardless of where the pen was, it was a devastating loss, one from which I thought I might not recover. Through my grief, however, I was able to devise a plan that would alleviate my sorrow. I surmised that if my brother gave me his pen, which he hardly ever used anyway, then he could have the pen out of the next box of cereal. He, of course, would have none of that plan, so I decided to plead my case to Mom and Dad, and all of my younger siblings. Promises of future favors gained the support of a couple of the younger ones, but I hit a brick wall with my parents.

They informed me that the pen belonged to my brother, and no matter how much I wanted it, he was under no obligation to surrender it to me. If I could convince him to give it to me, or trade for something I owned, or if we could agree on a selling price that I could afford, then I had a shot at getting the pen. Otherwise, I was out of luck.

Although I didn't realize it at the time, it was one of my first lessons in libertarianism. Most of us learn that lesson early in life. No matter how bad you want something, you don't have the right to just take it. Not even if you want it really bad. And not even if someone else has taken something from you. Most people accept that as a fact in their personal lives.

We seem to take a different attitude, however, when the government gets involved. People seem to believe if they want a park or a hiking trail bad enough, it's alright to authorize the government to take money from a person and build one. They've somehow developed the attitude that if they want a business to locate in their county or state, it's alright for the government to take somebody's money and give it to a business. People who wouldn't even consider taking something from their neighbors don't seem to raise too much opposition when the sheriff takes the neighbor's house so the county can auction it off in a tax sale.

The problem is, we can't give away something we don't have, and since we don't have the right to take someone's property just because we want it, how can we believe that we have the right to appoint the government to do it for us?

   At least that's my take on it.

Out on a limb

My old buddy Stinky Wilmont was, without a doubt, shoes off or shoes on, the best tree climber at Millville Grade School. Even the big knobby Hackberry that was the corner marker between the school playground, Summit Taylor's back lot, and Fred Harrison's corn field, and stood 15 feet to the first limb was no match for Stinky's prowess.

Most of Stinky's buddies, who fancied themselves accomplished tree climbers also, held a deep appreciation for his abilities. Bernice Hawkins, however, upon seeing Stinky up in the tree, would assume her duties as a Junior Volunteer Safety Patrol Captain and inform Principal Walters, who in turn would come out and unleash a torrent of invective against poor Stinky for climbing the tree, and against the rest of us for encouraging his behavior with our praise.

Afterwards, Stinky felt bad, his buddies felt bad, Principal Walters went back and joined the other

teachers in the furnace room/smoking lounge, and
Bernice went back to playing on the maypole and
keeping a watchful eye in case anybody started to
enjoy themselves again.

I never really understood why it bothered them so.
While our gang wasn't really into maypoles, we didn't
mind if Bernice and her friends enjoyed them. And
most of us were still at least a couple of years away
from taking up smoking full time, but it didn't bother
us too much that most of the teachers had the habit.
Besides, everybody knew that climbing trees wasn't
nearly as dangerous as maypoles and cigarettes.

That's one of the things that attracted me to the
Libertarian Party. I've never had a Libertarian tell me
I couldn't climb a tree. Or tell me I had to.

Many of the discussions I have about Libertarianism
involve peoples' concerns about what they think
Libertarians want to take away from them, and why
most of the time those people are wrong.

Libertarians are opposed to the *initiation* of force. That means if an adult decides to enter into an arrangement with another adult, or group of adults, and if that arrangement doesn't require force, then Libertarians probably aren't going to use force to keep you out of that arrangement.

If you choose to pool your retirement savings with another person's savings, or with a million other peoples' savings, and dole it out as the group sees fit, Libertarians have no desire to take that choice away from you. You get to choose how it's managed and who manages it. The only thing you won't get to do is force somebody else to join or fund your arrangement.

And if you want to join together with some people and invest in a new business that wants to come to your town, you can do that too. You just won't be able to force your neighbors to invest if they don't want to.

Libertarians aren't going to try to deprive you of your right to associate with whoever you choose to associate with, and they won't try to deprive you of your right to support any charity or project you deem worthy of support, as long as you remember that your neighbor may not share your feelings about the worthiness of a particular charity or project.

The only thing Libertarians will take away from you is the ability to initiate force against another individual.

And that's a heck of a lot less than what the government is taking away from you now.

Stinky and the Secret Spy Ring

Back in 1961, lunch at Millville Grade School was 27 cents. They would throw in a half-pint of Best Ever milk for an extra 3 cents. White, of course. Chocolate was a nickel. Every Monday, Mom would issue each of us $1.50, our share of the milk check, and we were set for the week.

Things worked out pretty well like that, except for the time that Stinky Wilmont talked me into buying his spy ring with the secret compartment. I mostly wound up with an empty belly and a green finger. It did, however, teach me a valuable lesson about the proper utilization of funds.

The Indiana Department of Transportation announced a while back that it was canceling or postponing many road projects because of a $2.1 billion shortfall over the next ten years. When you watch the numbers spin on the pump while filling your vehicle, you have to wonder how they could run out of money. But if you look at how that tax money is being spent, it's a little more understandable.

It seems reasonable to expect that road use taxes should be used for the construction and maintenance of public roads. At least it seems reasonable to me. Apparently it doesn't seem reasonable to the people we send to Washington. When Congress passed its $284 billion highway bill a couple of years ago, it managed to slip in some items that might not be considered road worthy. I'm not sure why $3 million of the taxes we pay on gasoline should support the Packard Museum in Warren, Ohio. Or why $4 million should be used to remove graffiti in Brooklyn (I thought people in Brooklyn liked graffiti). Or why $1.5 million should be used on horse trails in Virginia. In all, the highway bill spends billions of dollars on 4000 projects that have nothing to do with roads.

Not that my state was left out in the cold. The Children's' Museum in Indianapolis received $14 million. Even locally, we find gas and wheel tax money being spent on the Cardinal Greenway, a hiking path for people that like to hike, and the Red Tail Conservancy, a home for birds and frogs. No doubt worthy and commendable projects, but certainly not falling under the category of roads.

More and more, our elected officials in Washington seem to be losing their grip on fiscal responsibility, which is why I was happy to hear there is a movement in the works to reduce the federal highway tax from 18 cents per gallon to 2 cents per gallon, and allow the states to collect and spend the money where it belongs, on the roads.

It seems we stand a better chance of holding our state and local officials accountable for errant spending. That, or we could send Stinky Wilmont to Washington to give them a lesson or two on how to spend our money.

Swap Meat

There weren't a lot of extra-curricular activities when I attended Millville Grade School. Occasionally we would load onto Howard Tucker's bus and ride over to Ashland or Dalton for a softball game. Once in a while we would head over to Memorial Park for a picnic and to gather specimens for our leaf collections. I suppose students are still allowed to have picnics, but I imagine by now collecting leaves in the park without a permit of some sort would lead to a violation of some law or statute.

Our picnics consisted of bag lunches that we brought from home, mostly sandwiches and potato chips. This was back before peanut butter cost $8.00 a jar, when jelly was homemade, and before we knew how to spell bologna or what it was made from. It was a pretty safe bet what your bag was going to contain when it was time to eat.

But my old pal, Stinky Wilmont, drew a great deal of pleasure from convincing other students to swap lunches with him. He always found someone willing to make a trade, but I never saw the attraction. Regardless of what Stinky and the others were hoping for, they were still going to end up with a peanut butter and jelly sandwich, or a bologna sandwich. And no matter how many times you made the switch, the outcome was always the same.

Here in Indiana, our Governor and our state legislators have been involved in the same sort of swap fest over in Indianapolis for a while. After a great amount of public outcry and voter unrest over the property tax debacle, our lawmakers decided to make some changes. They have decided to collect a little less property tax and a little more sales tax. Some of them want to swap some elected officials for some appointed officials, and some elected assessors for some hired assessors. Some of them want to trade small government schools for large government schools.

Maybe their original plan might have been to make the unfair property tax a little less unfair, and to make the arbitrary assessment system a little less arbitrary, but their new plan still allows people living in identical homes and with identical incomes to pay different amounts of property taxes based on a person's age. And it allows identical homes in the same neighborhood to be taxed at different rates depending on who lives in the home.

The Governor and our legislators want us to believe that they can reduce our total tax bill without reducing their spending, or by moving that spending from one branch of government to another. That somehow a temporary decrease in property taxes coupled with a permanent increase in sales taxes, or that replacing elected bureaucrats with appointed bureaucrats can somehow make the bottom line that citizens pay to the government more affordable.

Sorry Governor, but like I used to tell Stinky, that's a bunch of baloney.

Harold the Frog

I'm sure we've all heard the old theory that if you put a frog in a pan of hot water, it will immediately jump out, but if you place a frog in a pan of warm water, and turn up the heat slowly, the frog will stay in the pan, no matter how hot it gets.

I can't testify for sure if that is true. I do remember one time in my younger days when my old buddy Stinky Wilmont and I decided to give the theory a test. One afternoon, over at Stinky's house, we filled his mother's stewing pot about half-way with warm water and put it on the kitchen stove.

The plan was that Stinky would put his pet frog, Harold, in the pot, and I would start turning the knob slowly upward until either Harold or Stinky couldn't stand it anymore.

Unfortunately, as was the fate of many of our adventures, it didn't turn out exactly as we had planned. As soon as Harold hit the water, he made a mad leap out of the pan, across the kitchen cabinets and behind the refrigerator. In our efforts to catch him, we knocked the pot of water over on the stove, and spent the next several minutes trying to outrun Mrs. Wilmont and that extra thick Redelman's Hardware Store yardstick that she kept around for just such occasions.

Thus ended our scientific experiment. We never figured out if the water was too hot right from the beginning, or if Harold just figured it was going to get too hot and decided to make good his escape before that happened. We seldom spoke of Harold after that day, and we never saw or heard from him again.

Government has a way of turning up the heat slowly whenever it institutes a new program, and the American people seem to be pretty accepting of such things, as long as things increase slowly enough. When the income tax was first initiated in 1862, it took 3% of most Americans' (in the north) income, except for the very poor or the very rich. It was eliminated 1872, shortly after the war was paid off.

When it was re-adopted in 1913, (most politicians consider permanently) it again started as a small percentage of income on a portion of the population. That percentage has slowly grown and fluctuated over the years, reaching as high as 94% on some incomes at the end of the Second World War, before settling at our current levels of nothing to 35%, depending on your income. Of course, a myriad of other taxes, such as sales and property tax, have also increased slowly and gradually so that most of us spend about half of what we make to support government services and programs.

Social Security worked out about the same way. It started out in 1936 claiming 1% from the employee and employer on the first $3000.00 of income. The plan was to slowly increase the maximum "donation" to 3% by each party. Had that remained true, even adjusting for inflation, the most you would pay today would be $700.00 per year. The government turned it up to $12,500. Slowly. Some of us even remember when the maximum Medicare deduction was $43.00 per year. The combined unfunded liability of both programs is now around $60 trillion.

There was a strong and growing opposition to the health care plan that was proposed in Washington a while back. Maybe because a lot of people thought it is too expensive right from the start. Maybe because a lot of people thought it was going to be even more expensive in the future.

Thomas Jefferson warned that it is the natural tendency of government to grow. It's also the natural tendency of government to turn up the heat.

I think even Harold knew that.

Uncle Pug

When I was a kid back at Millville Grade School, my old buddy Stinky Wilmont used to tell stories about his Uncle Pug. It seems he had a fondness for hard liquor, but according to Stinky, Uncle Pug knew his limit when he began to partake of spirits. The problem was he always passed out before he got to it.

We seem to have a similar problem with the federal debt. Anytime we get close to the limit, somebody moves it. And they move it pretty often anymore, about once a year, or there about. The most recent action to raise the limit is buried in a recent government bail-out bill, and puts the ceiling at over $14 trillion. For now.

It causes all sorts of problems, too. The National Debt Clock in Times Square, that displays the ever increasing debt, ran out of spaces a couple of years ago when the debt reached $10 trillion. Reports have it that its owners are working feverishly to design a clock that will register a quadrillion dollars. From the sounds of things coming out of Washington this week, they better start working a little faster.

Every year for the last 40 years, Congress has spent more than it has collected. That's the reason taxpayers pay over $400 billion just in interest on the national debt every year. It's a contributing factor to the dollar losing 90% of its value in the last 40 years.

The interest we pay on that debt is the 3rd largest single expense in the federal budget. Last year, it took all of the taxes paid by all of the individual taxpayers west of the Mississippi River just to pay that interest. But before all of us taxpayers east of the Mississippi get too smug, we need to remember one thing. This year it's our turn.

I suppose if were paying that interest to ourselves, and if you used a lot of imagination, you might come up with a way to put a positive spin on things, but even that is not the case. About 60% of the publicly held debt is held by foreign investors. And I'm not totally convinced that all of those investors have our nation's best interest at heart.

As it stands right now, every person in the United States owes about $37,400.00 as their share of the national debt. That's if you don't count the unfunded future commitments to Social Security and Medicare. That kicks it up to about $160,000.00 per person.

I don't know about you, but I think that's about my limit.

Rights vs. Abilities

Stinky Wilmont was the biggest kid in the 5th grade at Millville Grade School. I suppose his size could have been attributed to genetics. As I remember, his mother was a woman of rather large proportions, and his father, though not as rotund, was still a mountain of a man. At least they seemed pretty big to me at the time.

So that could have had something to do with Stinky's size. Or it could have been that he was 14 years old. Regardless of the reason, he was a looming figure in the classroom, the lunchroom and on the playground at recess. And if Stinky took a notion to lay claim to your new pencil or eraser, or if he decided he was going to take your cornbread and leave you with just the beans, that's pretty well the way things worked out.

For the most part I stayed on good terms with Stinky, so most of the time my school supplies and my lunch were safe. Still, I couldn't figure out why he had the right to do some of the things he did. When I got a little older, I figured out that he didn't have the right to do them. He only had the ability.

A couple of years ago, before the Indiana General Assembly adjourned for the year, they passed a few new laws that Hoosiers are going to have to deal with. One thing they did was reduce the number of drivers that are exempt from the seatbelt laws. The drivers of pick-up trucks are no longer exempt, unless you're farming or making certain deliveries. They also created another entitlement program, providing health insurance to families that make up to $40,000.00, and funded with an increase in cigarette taxes. Apparently with smokers in the minority, the assembly felt safe on this one. But, as the number of smokers decreases, or turn to black market cigarettes, it's anybody's guess as to who will be chosen to fund the program as revenues decrease and costs increase. Property owners certainly seem a likely target under the current crop of lawmakers.

The thing is, the government doesn't have the right to make any private citizen wear a seatbelt, anymore than it has the right to make an uninvolved citizen pay for that citizen's medical expenses if he is hurt in an accident. And it doesn't have the right to force one group of citizens to pay for another group's health insurance. Or entertainment. Or retirement.

As citizens, we can't give our government the right to do these things. We can only give them the ability. We can also take that ability away. And that's something we had better start thinking about before things get totally out of hand.

Relatively Speaking

I made the Honor Roll a few times back at Millville Grade School. More times than my old buddy Stinky Wilmont. I can't remember a single time that he made it. On the other hand, I'm hard-pressed to remember a time that Bernice Hawkins didn't make the Honor Roll. So I felt pretty good when I compared my academic prowess to that of Stinky. But I felt pretty dumb if I compared myself to Bernice.

I guess that's an example of things being relative. I always thought we were poor when I was a kid, and by a lot of standards I'm still poor today. Looking back, I guess we were a lot better off than a lot of people in the world, and looking around, I guess we still are today. Relatively speaking, of course.

Seems like a lot of things are that way. We had some really nice days in March. A lot nicer than most of the days we had in February, but not nearly as nice as most of the days we are going to have in June. And there are some pretty nice homes in our neighborhood. Not nearly as fancy as the homes in Beverly Hills, I suppose, but a heck of a lot nicer than the ones we've seen in Haiti over the last few years. Once again, everything's relative.

Americans have always held a fierce pride about being a free nation. And as a nation and a people, we've done a lot of fighting over the years to make sure we stayed that way. Sometimes with guns, sometimes with words, sometimes with armies, and sometimes with individuals.

And I think most Americans still consider themselves to be relatively free. Certainly the information the government is gathering from the current census isn't nearly as intrusive as the information some countries gather from their citizens. Unless you were one of those 2 million people that had to answer (under penalty of law) the long census form. And even then it wasn't as much as what some governments ask.

And unlike a lot of countries, here in America we are free to own property, provided, of course, that we pay our property taxes to the government every year. Otherwise, somebody else will be free to own it, and pay the taxes on it.

Here before too long, and at least for awhile, we will be free to choose which company we want to buy our health insurance from, even though we won't be free to choose what type of policy to buy, and even though we won't be free to choose not to buy it at all.

And we certainly don't have to show our papers to the police just because they ask to see them. Of course you do have to show them your driver's license if they catch you driving or riding without your seat belt. And if Senators Chuck Schumer and Lindsay Graham get their way, you'll have to show and verify your biometric Social Security card before you can get a job. Or get on an airplane. But that's all. Probably.

Back in 2004, Libertarian Presidential Candidate hopeful Gary Nolan came to Hagerstown and asked his audience if they could name 3 things that our government doesn't tax or regulate. Nobody could. I've had 7 years to think about it, and I still can't.

Just like I used to take comfort in the fact that I was getting better grades than Stinky was getting, it's easy to become complacent as a nation, and rationalize that even though we lose a little more freedom each time Congress convenes, we are still more free than a lot of people in the world. And it would be hard to argue that we aren't.

But my goal at Millville Grade School should have been to get the best grades possible, regardless of what kind of grades Stinky got.

And our goal as Americans should be to remain free, regardless of what other countries decide to do. And maybe get back up to 4 or 5 things that government doesn't tax or regulate.

That's Not Really What I Had Planned

I've done a fair share of whittling over the years, even though I was never very good at it. For those of you who weren't raised in the country, whittling (I believe the correct spelling and pronunciation is whittlin'), involves taking out your pocket knife, picking up a stick or a piece of wood, and shaving away on that stick or piece of wood until it resembles something else. Often my work resembled a smaller stick or a smaller piece of wood, although occasionally I might end up with a lump that might pass for a deformed creature of some type.

My main problem was, whenever I set out to whittle something, it always took on a shape of its own, and even though I knew what I was trying to do, it just never ended up quite like I had envisioned it.

That seems to happen a lot whenever our legislators set us up with a new tax. Back in 1987, the Indiana General Assembly created the County Economic Development Income Tax (CEDIT), which county councils could adopt if they so desired. The rules for the use of the money collected by this tax were spelled out in the Indiana Code. In simple terms, CEDIT funds could be used for "economic development projects" or for "capitol construction of most publicly owned facilities." Whether or not tax money should be used on privately owned projects is still a point of contention even among many non-libertarians, but that's the law for now, so that's how it's going to be until we get the law changed.

Of course, much like my whittlin', things don't always work out exactly like the lawmakers planned. In my county, Wayne, the funds were used to buy an $8000.00 desk for the president of the Economic Development Commission, that used $75,000.00 of the funds just to find him. A county to the south of us used $125,000.00 of CEDIT funds to pay for housing prisoners in other county jails.

A few of years ago, my hometown, Hagerstown, spent several thousand CEDIT dollars on the Legacy Project, which was purported to help the people of Hagerstown achieve their dreams. It was probably a nice project, but maybe a little lacking in economic development field.

Shortly after that, the Hagerstown Town Council spent $5000.00 of the CEDIT funds to pay the salary of Communities in Schools site coordinator for the Nettle Creek School Corporation, whose job is "connecting adults with students through such programs as adult mentorships and tours of local businesses."

I pretty much gave up whittlin' because things seldom turned out like I had planned. I wish we could convince our legislators to stop passing most of these laws for the same reason.

Tipping Points

Right after high school, I worked at a little factory in Hagerstown that made centrifugal clutches for mini-bikes and go-carts, trying to make enough money so I could get through my first year of college. I didn't make it on either count. Although I didn't much care for the tedious work, I did meet some interesting people who also worked there.

One was a young man who had just completed a tour of duty in Viet Nam. He wasn't much older than me in some ways. In some ways he was a lot older. He had a lot of stories. Some were funny, and some were scary. I asked him once if he ever got scared enough to run when the Viet Cong were shooting at him. He said he didn't, but then he added that he had already decided that if he was ever in a fire fight, and the lieutenant gave the order to "affix bayonets", he was heading for the back of the line, and beyond, as fast as he could go. We all have our tipping points. Apparently his was an affixed bayonet.

When I was a kid, my old buddy Stinky Wilmont had a billy goat that we would tie to a little wagon so that he could pull us around the chicken yard. For some reason he got tired of the game sooner than we did, and he would run through the fence or under the lilac bush until we fell out of the wagon, and then he would jump and carry on until the wagon came loose. Different tipping points, I guess. Maybe that's why it kept getting harder and harder to tie that goat to the wagon.

Moms and Dads usually have different tipping points. Most children figure out where that point is early on, although the point is subject to change depending upon the circumstances, and the most successful children figure that out, also. Grandparents, of course, often seem to lose the tipping point gene, at least in relationship to their grandchildren. I think that probably helps to shorten the tipping point of the parents.

Tipping points are affected by a lot of factors. Sometimes it depends on who is doing the tipping.

A lot of Republicans who didn't have a problem when President Bush was bailing out private businesses, rediscovered their conservative streak when President Obama took charge of the handouts. And for some reason, Second Amendment restrictions seem to be easier to accept when a supposed Second Amendment advocate endorses them.

President Obama's trillion dollar plan for a national health care program naturally met with opposition from the GOP members of Congress, but even some from his own party objected to the ultimate cost. Sometimes reality can be a contributing factor to reaching a tipping point.

Although I haven't seen a lot of evidence of it yet, I figure that sooner or later the increased cost of running the government and its ever increasing programs will push voters to their tipping point. Especially the ones that are pulling the wagon. And especially as more and more people get in the wagon to ride.

Sooner or later that's bound to get your goat.

Different Strokes

Stinky Wilmont was one of my best buddies back in the days at Millville Grade School. I probably ended up in more trouble than I should have whenever I followed his lead, but I also had a lot more fun than I would have if Stinky hadn't been around.

Occasionally though, Stinky would embark on some adventure that I felt pretty sure was destined to end in tears, and either my better judgment, or fear, would get the better of me, and I would decide to leave him to his own devices. As the years and grades passed, and my judgment got better, partly because some of my fears were well-founded, Stinky and I kind of drifted apart. It may have been in part also, because Stinky's judgment never really showed any signs of improvement. I don't think there was any animosity between us, just my realization that Stinky and I might not have the same goals or values.

When Indiana started its lottery, I remember a woman in town who was absolutely obsessed with it.

After she had nearly depleted the family checking and savings accounts, her husband contacted all of the places in town that sold lottery tickets, cashed checks, or loaned money, and told them that he would no longer be responsible for his wife's debts.

I don't know for sure how much legal weight his action carried. But if she couldn't control her habit, I guess this was a good first step instead of just jumping into a divorce. I don't know whatever became of the situation. I hope it all worked out for them.

A couple of years ago, the fiancée of accused Craigslist killer Phillip Markoff, decided it might be time to reconsider her decision to "stand by her man", cancel their upcoming nuptials, and move on with her own life. Probably a good move on her part, I think.

In their recent sessions, about twenty state legislatures have introduced or discussed resolutions re-declaring their sovereignty as states, and re-asserting the limited power the federal government is granted under the Constitution. The basis for these resolutions is the 10th Amendment of that Constitution, which declares that: "The powers not delegated to the United States by the Constitution, nor prohibited by it to the States, are reserved to the States respectively, or to the people."

Many years ago, Thomas Jefferson noted that "The natural progress of things is for liberty to yield and government to gain ground." It seems we've been pretty complacent over the years about yielding our liberties to an ever growing government. There aren't many things we can do anymore that don't require some sort of government permission or license. Even getting together to protest against the government often requires a permit from the government. And for the most part, it seems the American people have pretty well accepted that.

The renewed interest in State and personal sovereignty seems then to be more tied to the federal government's insatiable appetite for spending. It might be the official federal debt, which recently passed $14 trillion, or the unofficial debt (which includes the federal government's unfunded liabilities), which has been estimated at over $75 trillion. It might be the hundreds of costly mandates the federal government has, without Constitutional authorization, imposed upon the States. Perhaps there is finally a realization that all of this debt will eventually fall on the people of the States, and a realization that it is more debt than taxpayers can afford. Perhaps it's simply a common sense survival instinct that tells people to avoid things that will probably end up causing them harm.

Whatever the reasons, it may indeed be time for the States to take a critical look at where the federal government is leading them, and renegotiate their deal with that government.

Or at least make them abide by the old one.

When we got a little older...

Stinky's First Car

My old buddy Stinky Wilmont's first car was a hand-me-down his older brother, Leonard, had given to him. It was an Oldsmobile, as I remember, as big as a boat, with an engine so big he could pull a hay wagon if he wanted to. But usually he just put the hay in the back seat or the trunk.

One Saturday evening we were cruising town in Stinky's Olds and stopped in for a fill-up. This was back in the day when gas stations put the gas in for you. The attendant pumped for a while, and then walked up to Stinky's window and stated, "You're going to have to turn this car off, sir. It's gaining on me." I always figured the attendant was just being a smart-aleck, but that old car did take a lot of gas.

There is an unemployment fund in Indiana that employers pay into every week, and if an employee loses their job, they get to draw some money out of that fund until they find another job. A while back, the people taking money out of the fund started taking more out than the people putting in were putting in.

The fund was going broke, so Indiana started borrowing some of the money the federal government has borrowed in order to keep the fund funded.

I suppose that might work, except that the people taking money out the federal government are taking out more than the people putting in are putting in. Kind of like that Indiana unemployment deal.

Not that it's anything new. The federal debt, just like the federal government, has been gaining on us for years. In 1957, the federal debt stood at a paltry $219 billion. It's gained every year since, sometimes a little, and sometimes a lot. Right now it's past $14 trillion. And it's going to gain another $1.4 trillion this year. And next year. Maybe a little more.

$10 billion of that additional debt will come from Social Security paying out more than it takes in each year. It will gain on us a lot more when an additional 80 million people start drawing money out of it in the next ten years, and there isn't another 80 million people to keep putting money in.

The government seems to be gaining on us in a lot of areas. The Bureau of Labor Statistics recently reported that 430,800 people worked in factories in my state, Indiana, in January 2010. At the same time, 442,800 people worked for the government. That makes government the second largest employer in Indiana. It's just behind retailers and gaining fast. And not just in Indiana.

According to Assembly magazine, as recently as 1990, 21 states still had more manufacturing jobs than government jobs. Today, not one state can make that claim.

It didn't take my buddy Stinky too long to figure out that he couldn't afford that big Olds, and luckily he was able to get rid of it before it broke him, in favor of a more economical model that got him where he wanted to go for a lot less money.

I hope as a nation we should be so lucky.

Tolerable Differences

Stinky Wilmont was my best pal back when we were attending Millville Grade School. I guess we had a lot of things in common. We both thought Rin Tin Tin was a lot smarter and faster than Lassie, and we were convinced Popeye and Bluto could both have done a lot better than Olive Oyl . We didn't think much of the creamed peas they served us in the cafeteria on Wednesdays, and if the truth was told, neither one of us was really all that happy to be in school at all.

Of course, we had our differences, too. Stinky seemed to place a little less emphasis on personal hygiene. As I remember, that kind of ran in the family. He also liked to go coon hunting. I tried it a couple of times, but I just never saw the attraction.

It all worked out pretty well, though. We still got together when necessary to hide the creamed peas under the Best-Ever milk cooler, but I didn't try to make Stinky take a bath, and he didn't try to make me go coon hunting. It just seemed like the natural solution.

That philosophy has served me fairly well through the years. I've made friends that like to go hunting and friends that don't. I've made a few friends that don't like to bathe, although we're not really *that* close. I've made friends that share my religious beliefs, and friends that have different religious beliefs, and friends that have no religious beliefs. I have friends that drink alcohol and friends that don't, friends that smoke and friends that don't, and a couple friends that chew or dip snuff. As long as people are tolerant enough that no one tries to force their choices on someone else, we seem to get along pretty well, although I do pay closer attention to the wind direction when I'm around one of the chewers.

I think for the most part, Americans have usually behaved that way, at least in their personal dealings. That's not to say that some individuals aren't pretty insistent about bringing others around to their way of thinking, but for the last 150 years or so, even with some major differences in opinions, we've managed to keep things half-way civil.

One of the things that has set us apart from some countries around the world is the way we have handled our elections. No matter how nasty the campaign was, or how much difference there was in the ideologies, in the end, the loser steps aside and the winner takes office (except for a few local mayoral races, that is). It's not like that everywhere. In some countries the losers grab guns and start shooting at the winners. Not much tolerance, I guess.

I don't think we've reached that point in this country yet, although there does seem to be a growing divide among people concerning what they expect from their government. Right now there is a large group of people that want the government to provide health care for everybody. There's also a large group of people that don't want the government to provide health care for everybody. Although we haven't seen too many guns brought out yet, several people on each side of the debate are getting pretty insistent, and even downright nasty, trying to make sure that their side gets to make the rules.

Before we do get to that point, maybe we simply need to step back and allow the people who want government health care to go ahead and pay for government health care plan, and allow people who don't want government health care to go their own way.

I think that would work for a lot of government programs. At least it always worked for Stinky and me.

And while we're at it, you're all welcome to come to church with me next Sunday if you want to.

But nobody's forcing you.

Yet.

Guess Again

One of the highlights of the summer when I was growing up was the Mooreland Free Fair. Come to think of it, it's still one of the highlights of the summer. I suppose everybody that attends the fair has their own favorite attractions. My favorite is getting the chance to see old friends.

In my younger days, I spent a lot of time at the fair with my old buddy, Stinky Wilmont. One of Stinky's favorites every year was the Gypsy Weight Guesser. Stinky had what might be called an unusual shape, and he was convinced that it threw the Weight Guesser off of his game. Stinky would give the man a quarter, and the man would take a guess about his weight. He always missed by more than the allowable margin, and Stinky would laugh and walk away with a prize that was probably worth a nickel on the high side.

Still, it was Stinky's quarter, and Stinky's choice to

spend it. No matter how bad of a guesser the old man was, Stinky didn't care, the old man didn't care, and I certainly didn't care. Stinky got a prize, the old man got a quarter, and everybody was happy.

There's still a lot of guessing going on. I read the other day that somebody had determined that the earth's atmosphere weighs 5 quadrillion tons. Now, maybe it does, and maybe it doesn't. They could have guessed 4 quadrillion tons, or 6 quadrillion tons, and I doubt that anybody would have offered much of an argument. At least I know I wouldn't.

Sometimes bad guessing ends up costing us money, though. A while back someone guessed that 250,000 people use the Cardinal Greenway walking and bicycling trail every year. Given the number of decent days in a year and the number of people that you see on the trail on any one of those decent days, I'm guessing that they guessed high. The 250,000 number was used to justify using our road taxes on the Greenway, I guess.

In Wayne County a couple of years ago, the director of tourism guessed that a new convention center in Richmond wouldn't compete with existing businesses that offer meeting rooms for various functions. I guess she was trying to convince those existing businesses to support the new tax that would finance the new center. I guess it didn't work.

When Governor Mitch Daniels was working for George Bush, his best guess was that the Iraq War would cost the United States $50 billion. $60 billion, tops. Guess again.

Back in 2008, Congress passed, and President Bush signed, a new housing bill. It put taxpayers on the hook for all of the bad loan decisions that mortgage brokers Fannie Mae and Freddie Mac have made in the past, or may make in the future. The government is guessing it could cost taxpayers $25 billion, but in reality there is no limit on the amount of bad loans that the American taxpayer might be required to buy.

There aren't very many government programs that don't end up costing more than the government guessed they would cost, or that turn out the way the government guessed they would turn out. I don't guess that's going to change as long as we keep putting the same people in charge.

I guess a lot of people think that elected officials somehow have a better understanding on how to manage and spend your money as soon as they get into office.

I guess I don't believe that.

Wanna Bet?

Several years ago, the poker club I belonged to needed a substitute player for the evening. Although I had a few reservations about it, we invited my old buddy, Stinky Wilmont, to sit in for the evening. Years before, Stinky had a knack for swindling me out of my lunch money back at Millville Grade School, but I was little older and feeling a little smarter by this time, so I figured it was time to forgive and forget, and maybe get some of my lunch money back.

We played 'dealers choice', which meant that the dealer chose the game for that hand. That worked out pretty well most of the time, since the dealer normally chose 5 or 7 card stud, or a simple variation of one of those games. On this particular evening, however, when the deal came around to Stinky, he called out "Oklahoma 7 card no peek, high card up and low card down wild".

He then dealt the cards as he explained the rules, as the rest of us anted and bet and hoped for the best. When the dealing and the betting ended, I was grinning like a possum as I showed my four aces and prepared to rake in the pot. That's when Stinky informed us that red fours were also wild, and since he had two of them, he had a straight flush and that I had finished second. We voted not to invite Stinky to our game again.

But that's not what I wanted to write about today. In 1987, the Indiana General Assembly created the County Economic Development Income Tax (CEDIT), which county councils could adopt, if they so desired. The rules for the use of the money collected by this tax were spelled out in the Indiana Code. In simple terms, CEDIT funds could be used for "economic development projects or for capitol construction of most publicly owned facilities."

Whether or not tax money should be used on privately owned projects is still a point of contention even among many non-libertarians, but until we get the law changed, those are the rules.

But sometimes, our government doesn't play by the rules. In Wayne County, the Economic Development Commission used $75,000.00 of CEDIT funds just to find someone to serve as their president, and pay for his move to Richmond. And another $8000.00 to buy him a desk.

In Union County, the county commissioners used CEDIT funds, $125,000.00 worth, to pay for housing prisoners in other counties. Now, I'm sure a president needs a desk, and I know prisoners need a place to stay, but you can't pay for it with CEDIT funds. Not unless you change the rules.

We run into the same dilemma when the politicians collect our road use taxes, then change the rules and spend them on the Erie Canal Museum.

Or when they set the federal debt limit at $14 trillion, and when the debt reaches that limit, then raise the debt limit to $15 trillion.

Or when they swear to uphold the Constitution of the United States when they are elected, but then decide that the first ten amendments of that Constitution might be a little too restrictive to suit their needs, and might need to be more loosely interpreted.

A lot of people would have a hard time keeping their taxes paid and believing politicians even if the government played fair. It gets even harder when they keep changing the rules.

I haven't seen Stinky Wilmont for a long time, and I'm not sure what he's doing now. But I suspect he might be working for the government.

Ugly Cars and Pretty Women

Car companies have designed and manufactured a lot of different styles of cars over the years. Some I thought were really sharp. Some I thought were too ugly to drive down the street. Back in my younger days, when I paid more attention to such things, and thought it mattered more, AMC seemed to have the corner on the ugly car market. The Pacer and Gremlin come to mind.

Last week a buddy of mine was showing me a new car that he had just purchased. It was some kind of an electric and gas combination, really tiny, and certainly not very attractive, in my mind, anyway. But I guess he liked it, just like the people that bought Pacers and Gremlins liked Pacers and Gremlins.

I kind of had the same feelings about my old buddy Stinky Wilmont's girlfriend, Rowena. An awful, spiteful woman, mean-spirited and bossy, and just a touch on the plain side. Still, Stinky thought the world and all of her, and I guess that was what mattered.

The saving grace in these instances was that I didn't have to buy a Pacer or a Gremlin if I didn't want to. I didn't even have to ride in one if I didn't want to, and to the best of my memory, I never did. Neither did I have to date Rowena, or even hang out with Stinky when Rowena was around. It seemed like a pretty workable solution, to me, anyway.

I'm thinking that maybe when the Founding Fathers put our Constitution together, a few of them may have had a buddy like Stinky, who had a girlfriend like Rowena. After they decided and listed specifically what duties the federal government would have, and what specifically it would be allowed to do, they tacked on the 10th Amendment, which states ***"The powers not delegated to the United States by the Constitution, nor prohiblted by it to the States, are reserved to the States respectively, or to the people."***

Again, sounds like a pretty workable solution to me. The government takes care of its enumerated duties, and we get to decide how to handle the rest of our business. While our founders may not have been able to foresee every issue that might arise, they seemed to realize that a central government probably wouldn't always be able to come up with programs that suited everyone in the country.

Not that it hasn't tried. Currently, the federal government is working feverishly, amid occasional setbacks, to come up with a health care plan that will work for everyone in the country. We all know that it's not going to be able to come up with such a plan, and it wouldn't be a big deal, if, like AMC and its ugly cars, the American people could take it or leave it. But again, we all know that's not going to happen. That's not how the government works.

Somewhere along the line, the federal government decided that it was no longer going to honor the 10th Amendment, and then somewhere along the line most of the states and people decided that was okay, and pretty soon the federal government began to believe that it has the authority to dictate any solution to any problem it thinks we might have.

Fortunately, there is a growing movement among many people and states to reaffirm their 10th Amendment protections. Regarding the feds growing involvement in education, health care, gun rights, and the exploding debt that accompanies an ever growing government, people are looking for ways to simply say, "thanks, but no thanks".

I saw a t-shirt one time that read, "Life is too short to dance with ugly women." I don't know about that, but it is too short to drive ugly cars.

And it's way too short to let the government run it.

Can You Dig It

My buddy Marvin, a farmer up by Mooreland, is fond of telling the story about the time he added a new hired-hand, Wilburn, to help with some summer projects around the farm. It was mid August, and one of the projects involved installing a new roof on one of his barns. When Marvin took the new man out to the barn, Wilburn informed him that he wasn't able to climb.

Marvin ensured him that wasn't a problem because there was plenty of other work that needed to be done. They then drove to the other end of the farm, where a new fence needed to be built. Wilburn was given a set of posthole diggers, and instructed where the holes for the end posts needed to be dug. If you've ever built much fence, you probably remember how hot the sun gets and how hard the ground gets around mid August.

When he returned home for lunch, Marvin saw the posthole diggers leaning up against the barn and

Wilburn nailing shingles on the roof. To this day, Marvin maintains that one of his greatest accomplishments in life was teaching the new man how to climb.

We've all been in situations where we found out we were capable of doing something we didn't think we were capable of doing. A few times in my youth, I was convinced I couldn't possibly get out of bed so early in the morning to milk cows. My father was able to convince me otherwise.

A while back, I was involved in a discussion about an employee who was taking a $3.50 per hour pay cut, in order to relocate with a company that offered health insurance. I offered my opinion that with an extra $140.00 per week, a person could buy a high-deductible major-medical policy, open a tax deductible medical savings account, and in the long and short run be money ahead. The general consensus among the group was that people wouldn't be able to make themselves contribute to the savings account.

I suggested that maybe they needed to have a talk with my Dad.

The American people have developed quite a list of things they think they can't do. The recent economic downturn and resultant budget cuts have caused some cities and towns to consider eliminating government provided trash pick-up. A lot of people are convinced that if the government doesn't provide the service, trash will pile up and eventually bury us all. But in actuality, there are people who pay for their own trash pick-up, or haul their own trash, with seemingly minimal side effects.

At the federal level, the stakes are a little higher, but the principle is the same. We've known for a long time that the Social Security and Medicare systems are paying out more money than they are collecting, and the state of the economy is speeding those systems respective demise. The keepers of the programs recently estimated that Medicare is just 8 years away from financial meltdown, with Social Security meeting the same fate 20 years later.

With so many people convinced that they can't survive without a government run retirement and healthcare system, I'm sure we'll see a lot of activity by the government in the next few years trying to make those systems work by raising taxes, lowering benefits, raising qualifications, and lowering expectations.

I'd like to believe that the people who will come out winners in all of this are the ones who are able to figure out that they can take care of themselves, and their retirement, and their healthcare, without a lot of interference, or help, from the government.

Unfortunately, the way things have been working out lately, they'll end up being the ones who take care of the people that couldn't, or wouldn't, figure it out.

Go figure.

Merry Christmas
and
Happy New Year

A collection of holiday thoughts

(sort of)

I'm Sorry, Did You Say Something?

One of my favorite pastimes in my younger days was devising new ways to irritate my little sisters. At one point, my old buddy Stinky Wilmont and I discovered that simply peering at one of them over the back of a school bus seat was enough to set them off. We, of course, were delighted, until one Sunday morning when we were taking the family station wagon to church. I summoned my best staring technique, and proceeded to look at two of my sisters at the same time. I fully expected a swat from the front seat when they screamed in unison, "Mom!!!!!...he's looking at us!!!!" Instead, our Mother calmly replied, "Well, just ignore him."

I was crushed that our diabolical plan to drive my sisters stark raving mad could be so easily neutralized, and I worried what effect 'just ignoring me' would have on my other methods of aggravation. It turned out to be an effective deterrent against most of our audio and visual taunts, and Stinky and I eventually reverted to catching crawdads as an alternate form of entertainment.

That little piece of advice worked out pretty well for my sisters then, and it has served me quite well since. I also think it would have come in handy out at the statehouse a while back. The ACLU was involved in another lawsuit seeking a court order to prevent anybody from opening a legislative session with a prayer. Now, I understand that there are people, both religious and secular, who are opposed to intermixing government and religion. And if anybody attempts to force an unwilling person to pray, we should all join with the ACLU and make sure the courts stop it. But it seems we have become dependent on the courts and the government to shield us from everything that might offend us, and we're talking about something here that doesn't require a court order or government intervention of any kind. If a person doesn't want to participate or listen to a prayer, simply use the time to organize your own thoughts, or get a cup of coffee, or reflect on some lesson you learned from your mother early in life.

I'm not sure when we developed such thin skin. High schools and colleges have changed the names of their team mascots for fear they might offend certain groups of people, usually Native Americans. (Fortunately for my Alma Mater, the animal kingdom is not so touchy about these things.) And if my old buddy Stinky was still in school today, I just imagine he would be subjected to some sort of counseling to help him deal with the possible trauma of having such a nickname.

Americans aren't the only people that could stand a little toughening up. Recently a teacher in Sudan was sentenced to 15 days in jail for allowing her students to name a teddy bear after a religious leader. And in Australia, Santa has been instructed not to say, "Ho, Ho, Ho!" on the chance that certain professional ladies might take offense.

Now, just so you know, the holiday season is approaching, and if I meet you on the street, I might wish you a Merry Christmas. If that offends you, feel free to ignore me. If it <u>really</u> offends you, and you feel the necessity to chastise me for making such a comment, or if you feel the need to make some unsavory gesture in my direction, that's alright too. I'll probably just ignore it.

And just in case I don't see you before then, Merry Christmas. Ho, Ho, Ho.

You say you want a Resolution

It's not that I have anything against New Year's Resolutions. I know that sometimes people stick to them, and sometimes things work out. Thirty years ago a resolution and a couple of $100.00 side bets got me off of cigarettes. Then, after a couple of false starts, I gave up alcohol and chewing tobacco, and I'm getting along pretty well with a couple of last year's promises. I've made peace with the neighbor's cat, and I hardly ever bring up farm subsidies or politics with my in-laws. Unless they mention it first. Or unless somebody does something really stupid. All in all, I'm really doing pretty well, I think.

But some resolutions are tougher to keep than others. Some resolutions require almost super human determination. Sometimes we need a little help, sometimes we need another plan, and sometimes we just need a little creative score keeping. That's what I've decided to do with my resolution this year. I've been watching Congress and its imaginative budgeting, and I think I can make their system work for me.

Congress has developed a system by which they can spend more than they did last year and still call it a spending cut. I don't understand how it works for sure, but apparently, if they don't spend as much as they could have spent, that qualifies as a spending cut, they get to brag about it, and the taxpayers are supposed to be grateful. I haven't figured out how spending cuts could have allowed our federal budget to double and our national debt to quadruple in the last 15 years, but I guess our lawmakers thought it was working well enough to vote themselves a raise a while back.

I don't know if they saved enough with their spending cuts to send $200 billion (that's $400,000.00 for each of the 500,000 displaced families) to Louisiana after the 2005 hurricane, or $284 billion to help fund 14,000 pork barrel projects that our congressmen depend on to win re-election, but I guess they think they did. It really doesn't matter because I don't think they ever planned on balancing the budget or paying off the debt anyway.

But back to my New Year's Resolution. I used to make a pledge to lose weight every year. This year I resolve to try not to gain as much weight as I did last year, unless I go over to Mom's too many times for chicken and dumplings, or my wife makes one of those red velvet cakes with that fluffy white icing, or our friend and neighbor, Helen, brings over one of those strawberry rhubarb pies with that criss-crossed crust with sugar sprinkled on it.

So that's my resolution for this year, and I'm feeling pretty darned good about it.

I think I'll have a cookie.

A Long Weight

It's New Year's Resolution time again, and good intentions will be thicker than presidential candidates in Iowa for the next few days. My resolution will be to take off a few pounds. I figure sooner or later, if I make it often enough, I'll surely drop at least a couple of pounds.

When I graduated from high school, I weighed in at about 140 pounds. Now, over 40 years later the bathroom scales are spinning towards 200 and screaming for mercy, and the waist and inseam measurements on my pants have traded places since my school days.

I'm not sure when I gained all the weight. I guess like so many things in my life, it crept in an ounce or two at a time, gradually, so as not to alarm me. I compensated by letting my belt out a notch and wearing it a little lower, and convincing myself that I was simply maturing as part of the natural process. Still, if someone would have asked me 40 years ago if

I would like to pack around an extra 60 pounds all day, I'm pretty sure I would have told them no.

Over the last several years we've been experiencing the same creep from our government. While we were busy raising our families and buying groceries, it has continued to grow. Sometimes it grows by ½ of a percent in the form of an economic development income tax, or 1 percent as a sales tax increase. Sometimes it grows a little faster, like with a property tax increase, and we will throw a fit for just a little while, and the government will tax somebody else for a little while to placate some of the property owners, but it will continue to grow.

When I graduated from high school the national debt stood at $389 billion. That amount won't pay the interest on the debt as it stands today. It didn't get that way overnight, but every year since I graduated the federal government has spent more than it has confiscated. Sooner or later that's bound to catch up with you.

The bureaucracy is growing in other ways as well. Last summer, a friend of mine was informed that he would have to get permission from his neighbors before he could add a room onto the back of his house. Down the road a piece, a grandson was ticketed for carrying a bow and arrows on his grandfather's farm. In the next couple of years, the light bulbs that you are likely using to read this book will be illegal and will need to be replaced with bulbs that can cost 6 times as much.

Someone asked me once if I could name three things that the government didn't tax or regulate. It was a tough question then, and it's getting tougher every year. It's going to get a lot tougher if we don't start paying attention.

It didn't take any effort for me to put on this extra weight, but it will take a lot of effort to get it off. The same is true of the government. Thomas Jefferson said that it is the natural tendency for government to grow and for liberty to yield. It won't take any effort at all on our part for government and taxes to grow.

It will take a lot of effort on our part to reduce our government back to its intended size and purpose. And it will take a lot of effort to keep it that way.

   That's how it works when you battle natural tendencies.

Christmas Cards or Credit Cards

My wife informed me the other day that we are cutting back on our Christmas spending this year. Sounds like a good plan to me, although I've decided to take a wary "I'll believe it when I see it" approach to the whole deal. There's always the possibility that I'll end up being a real schmuck on Christmas morning if I over-estimate what "cutting back" actually means, maybe even worse than the time I bought her a pant suit that was two sizes too big. Or the time I bought her a new can opener that was just like the one I had given her the Christmas before.

We never have been ones to go overboard buying presents. Socks and underwear have always been a staple. Our children and grandchildren have probably fared better than some and worse than others, but we've never bought anything for Christmas that we couldn't pay for at the time. It seems to work out better that way, and it certainly makes January and February a lot more tolerable.

I've heard of people that were still paying for last year's presents when they started buying this year's presents. I imagine that has to take some of the joy out of giving. Credit and credit cards seem to be the major culprits in the deal. People tend to lose track of what they're spending if they don't have to fork over the cash on the spot. A study by Debt.com found that people who pay with credit cards tend to spend about 25% more than people who pay with cash. And then there's that interest thing to contend with.

It's beginning to look a lot like Christmas up in Washington, too. They don't really have a pay as you go system in place up there anymore, and you just about have to believe that our representatives have lost track of how much they're spending. Our national debt passed $14 trillion sometime back, but that's only if you don't add in our future obligations to Social Security, Medicare, and Medicaid. That kicks it up to $60 or $70 trillion, give or take a trillion or two.

Like people who charge more on their credit cards than they pay on the bill each month, the government is spending and adding to the debt more than it is paying on it. By about a trillion dollars a year. And just like those people with their credit cards, it doesn't make it any easier when you have to pay all of that interest, which in the government's case is over $1 billion per day.

Of course, we all know that government doesn't actually pay anything on the debt. Taxpayers do. And right now they're also paying a lot of interest. In fact, 40 cents of every dollar of individual income taxes collected goes just to pay interest. And it doesn't appear that the government is being overly frugal with the 60 cents that's left over, either.

We also know that we aren't going to be able to pay off this debt. We are going to hand it over to our children and grandchildren. In 10 years it ought to be up around $22 trillion.

If we don't add anymore spending. And if nobody else loses their job.

Thomas Jefferson had some excellent advice years ago when he said that "It is incumbent on every generation to pay its own debts as it goes." Sounds like a good idea to me all year, not just at Christmas.

And if you want to get the kids a little something extra this year, slip a bill in each of their stockings for $39,118.00. That's each ones share of the federal debt. And be sure to remind them that just like the socks and underwear, it's gonna be even bigger next year.

Merry Christmas.

Promises and Resolutions

I ran into my old buddy Stinky Wilmont the other day, and in the course of our conversation, the subject of New Year's resolutions came up. I asked Stinky if he was going to make any, and he replied that this year, he was going to resolve to gain 20 pounds and acquire a few more credit cards.

When I pointed out that those resolutions ran afoul of conventional resolutions, Stinky said that he realized they did, but that he had never had much luck with plans that involved losing weight or trimming his budget. He said he thought he would feel better about himself if he could keep whatever resolutions he made, and since gaining weight and spending money kind of came naturally for him anyway, it just seemed like the logical way to go.

I started to explain to him that those resolutions probably weren't in his best long term interest, but Stinky didn't tend to think that far ahead. Besides, resolutions are kind of like promises to yourself by yourself, so Stinky's resolutions probably weren't any of my business, anyway.

But there is a difference between resolutions and promises. For years, politicians have been getting elected by making promises to the voters. A lot of those promises were about money. Sometimes they promised money they didn't really have yet. Sometimes they had the money and spent it on something they had promised to somebody else. Sometimes they never had the money at all. Most of the time they were promising somebody else's money anyway.

That's what happened down in Prichard, Alabama. A while back, Prichard told about 150 city retirees that the city didn't have enough money to pay them the pensions they were promised. They can still find the people that made the promises, but apparently they're having trouble finding the people that will keep them.

Prichard, Alabama is just one of many entities across the country that has made promises it cannot keep.

Public employee pensions have promised $3.2 trillion that they don't have. Social Security and Medicare are in the same shape, but on a larger scale, and every day, another 10,000 citizens will turn 65, and get in line for their share of the promises the government made, and hope there are still enough people around willing to keep those promises somebody else made for them.

Over the next few years, we are going to hear a lot of stories about pension plans from all levels of government that have run out of money. Most of the problems will be the result of the government making promises to other people for other people.

We could solve a lot of those problems if we could just take on some personal responsibility, and start making and keeping our own promises.

Maybe that would be a good New Year's resolution for all of us.

Right, Stinky?.....Stinky?..........Stinky?

Sorry, Virginia

I absolutely love watching my grandchildren interact with Santa Claus. From their first Christmas, they all started out not wanting to have much to do with him, but by last Christmas, they were comfortable enough to sit on his lap and place their orders, except for Dawson, who even this year prefers to shout his requests from a safe distance. I wonder how long it will be before once again they decide they don't want much to do with Santa.

Many years ago, on one particular Christmas, I remember receiving a CO_2 Gas Powered Crossman BB and Pellet Rifle. It had a wooden butt and fore stock, and a canvas sling, and was, I believed at the time, the most powerful weapon mankind had ever created. I couldn't believe my good fortune when I opened it on Christmas morning.

When I circled it and wrote my name next to it in the Sears-Roebuck catalog, it was just something to dream about. I was long past the age of believing in Santa Claus, and I knew it was too expensive for Mom and Dad to buy for me, being that there were 7 other brothers and sisters figuring in on the equation.

Still, even though I knew Santa and his Elves didn't magically make it appear, I was awful happy to have it, and I didn't give much thought to what it took for my parents to get it for me, or whether I'd even done anything to deserve it. All things considered, I probably appreciate it more now than I did even then.

I don't know when I came to the conclusion that Santa wasn't real, but I've come to realize that apparently a lot of people in this country, in addition to my grandkids, still believe that he exists.

That might be because our government has been playing Santa Claus for a number of years. It's been giving away a lot of money to a lot of people. And as long as a lot of people were handing a lot of money over to the government, things went along pretty well. The problem started when it began handing out more than it took in. So far it's handed out about $14 trillion more than it's taken in.

I read an article the other day about a 55 year-old government employee who is retiring after Christmas this year. A shot at a 40 year-long retirement is a pretty nice gift by most standards. Unfortunately, many of the funds that were set up to pay for some of those long term retirements have been left severely underfunded because of our government's tendency to give away gifts it really couldn't afford to give away. Indiana's Public Employee Retirement Fund alone is short by about $10 billion. Publicly funded retirement accounts across the nation are estimated to be short by about $4 trillion.

The government would have us believe that if we wish real hard somebody will replace the missing money in those accounts. And somebody probably will. But it won't be Santa Claus. Every time the government gives away another gift, or borrows and spends another dollar, it hands the bill to the taxpayers.

It doesn't really matter if our grandchildren continue to believe in Santa Claus for a while longer, but since a whole lot of baby boomers are ready to get in line, it would behoove both the gift givers and the gift receivers to take a reality check.

And the sooner, the better.

Decisions, Decisions, Decisions

John Mellencamp had a pretty tough New Year's resolution to keep a couple of years ago. I've always been a fan of his music, if not his politics, so I was glad to hear his resolution that he was going to quit smoking. Maybe. Apparently, John agreed that if his son could get a million people to sign up as friends on the cyber community, Face book, he would give up cigarettes. As plans go, I guess this sounds like a good one. I'm not sure if his decision would be different if 2 million people asked him to continue smoking.

I quit smoking about 30 years ago on New Year's Day after I bet a couple of buddies $100.00 each that I could. We all three made the same bet. Turns out I was the only one that collected. And it's not that I didn't appreciate the motivation, or the $200.00, but in my later years I've often wondered why good ideas can't seem to stand on their own merits. If it was a good idea for me to quit smoking for $200.00, wasn't it just as good of an idea to quit for $20.00, or for nothing? I think I would have gone ahead and quit even if someone else had offered me $300.00 to continue, but I guess I'll never know for sure. Nobody offered.

Anyway, I was pulling for Mr. Mellencamp to get a million people to agree that he ought to quit. But if he really wants to quit, I hope he would do it for half a million people. Or maybe just because his son asked him to. Or better yet, just because he thinks it is a good idea.

I'd like to see a lot of people make a resolution to do the right thing just for the sake of doing the right thing more often. I'm not sure basing our decision on what most other people think or do, or what seems to be the most profitable, is always the best way to go.

Many years ago my Mom warned me about jumping off the bridge just because my friends did. I considered it sage advice, although thankfully it was never needed. (I did follow Stinky Wilmont out of the hay mow in an unthinking moment of distraction once, although it wasn't nearly as high as the bridge, and besides, that is a story for another time.)

A couple of years ago Senator Ben Nelson of Nebraska decided to vote for the health care bill after being offered $100 million for his state. Now, I'm not a big fan of government involvement in the health care business. I'm even less of a fan of this newest intrusion. And I do understand that there are people who genuinely believe that it is a good idea. But I have to wonder, if everybody in the country who is opposed to the bill would have passed the hat and offered Mr. Nelson $150 million, could we have headed this thing off?

I know that sometimes the majority is right, and sometimes the majority is wrong. And sometimes I agree with the majority and sometimes I don't. I suppose it's possible that one person could be right while everybody else is wrong, just like it's possible that one person could be wrong while everybody else is right.

However it works out, I resolve to spend the rest of the year doing what I think is right. As for Senator Ben Nelson, as far as I'm concerned he can go jump off the bridge.

More Thoughts

on

Less Government

Great Expectations

The California Second District Court of Appeals awhile back upheld the decision to award a man $2.4 million because of some sexual harassment that occurred at his work place. Apparently the man was offended by it, and didn't feel like he should be subjected to such treatment on the job. I'm sure a lot of people would feel that way.

I think he was expecting a little more money, though. The initial award from the jury was $18.4 million.

On the other hand, Linda, down at the coffee shop, says if it wasn't for the sexual harassment, she wouldn't even bother to show up for work. I suppose we all have different expectations in our lives.

Back at Millville Grade School, my old pal Stinky Wilmont was tickled if he managed to get a C on his report card. In gym. I felt the same way if I managed to pull off a B, but that snooty Bernice Hawkins expected to get A's in everything.

When I order a cheeseburger, I'd like for the lettuce to be at least some shade of green, and I hope that the bun isn't. Other than that, I'm not too picky. I do know a person that almost always sends her meal back to the kitchen for a redo at least once when the waitress brings it out. Again, different expectations.

The outcome of our elections are influenced greatly by peoples' expectations of what their government should do for them. Some people expect a lot. Others, not so much.

Being a Libertarian, I'm one of those that doesn't expect a lot. Libertarians think government should exist to protect its citizens from force and fraud. We'd like our road use taxes spent on roads, and the taxes we pay for education spent on education. And if you're not bothering somebody else, we think the government ought to leave you alone. As I said, we don't expect a lot.

Unfortunately, at least for the limited government crowd, people who don't expect much have been in the minority for the last several elections. At one time, people were pretty much expected to take care of their own retirement. Then, at some point, people started expecting the government to take care of part of their retirement. We've now reached the point where a whole lot of people expect the government to take care of all of their retirement.

People used to expect banks to make loans to people that could afford to pay them back. Now they expect banks to make loans to people that can't afford to pay them back, and then they expect the government to bail-out the bank and the borrower when the deal falls through.

Not too long ago, people expected businesses to provide a product or service for consumers, and expected them to succeed or fail based on their ability to figure out which product or service the consumers wanted, and how to provide that product or service at a profit. Now they expect the government to spend trillions of dollars on businesses that couldn't figure out either.

The problem is, expecting government to pay for our every wish costs a lot of money. The national debt doubled in the last eight years, and it's on course to more than double again in the next eight years. We're handing a multi-trillion dollar debt down to our grandchildren and great-grandchildren.

I'm just not sure they're expecting it.

Summit, Stinky, and Sisyphus

Summit Taylor was the janitor, groundskeeper, and sometimes recess monitor at my alma mater, Millville Grade School. He lived just across the fence on the other side of the big pile of leavings where he dumped the ashes from the coal furnace in the basement of the school building. One day at recess, my old buddy Stinky Wilmont decided to pick up a clinker out of that pile and see if he could throw it over Summit's garage.

Although Stinky didn't have enough arm to get the clinker over the roof, he did have enough power to get it to one of the windows on the building. Needless to say, Summit was not impressed with the feat. Neither was Principal Walters, and the entire 3rd and 4th grades were forced to stay in for the next two recesses because of Stinky's transgression.

I didn't have any concrete ideas on what constituted justice back then, but I was pretty sure the entire classroom didn't deserve to be punished because of Stinky's bad judgment. But, being in the 3rd grade and scared to death of a trip to Mr. Walter's office, I suffered in silence with the rest of my roommates, and wondered what misery Stinky would visit on us in the future.

As I grew older, and started questioning the accepted social order, I often wondered what would have happened if all of the students who had done nothing wrong, would have simply stood up and walked out when the recess bell rang. Probably the teacher would have told the principal, and probably the principal would have lined us all up for a paddling. But I still think we would have been right, and the teacher and principle would have been wrong.

Later on in school, while studying Greek mythology, we learned the story of Sisyphus. It seems Sisyphus had displeased a couple of the Greek gods and was sentenced to the task of rolling a huge boulder up a mountain, only to have it roll back down the mountain just before he reached the top. So Sisyphus would walk back down the mountain and start again. Forever.

I always wondered why Sisyphus didn't just step aside, let the rock roll down the mountain, and go on about his business. Probably wouldn't have made as good of a story, I guess. But as I remember it was an awfully big rock. And it was an awfully tall mountain.

We're getting ready to add a few trillion dollars to our federal debt. That debt already stands at over $14 trillion, or about $35,000.00 of debt for every man, woman and child in the United States. But that's just the debt the government likes to report. According to David Walker, past chairman of the Government Accountability Office, the unfunded liabilities of numerous government programs push the actual federal debt past $50 trillion, putting each citizens debt at over $160,000.00.

Of course, that is assuming that we all share the debt equally. We know that isn't the case, of course. Every year, of the 115 million Americans that file income tax returns, about 46 million don't pay any income tax at all. That leaves over $724,000.00 of debt for each of the people that do pay. Maybe a little less as long as the other 46 million continue to at least kick in for the Social Security debt. And the debt we don't get paid rolls over to our grandchildren. At least the ones that will be working and paying taxes.

Which gets me to wondering, could we really blame future generations if they decide they aren't going to pick up the bill for our ridiculously exorbitant spending policies? After all, they haven't done anything wrong, and we are handing them an awfully large rock.

And an awfully tall mountain.

Banjo and Stinky

There used to be a guy up in Mooreland who went by the nickname "Banjo". I don't know why people called him by that name. There were a lot of people with nicknames when I was growing up, but I didn't always know where the names originated. I was pretty sure how Stinky Wilmont got his name, and Fat Brown was pretty well self explanatory, as was Slim, Blubber and Shorty. I'm not so sure about Ginky, or Crowbar, or Skeeter.

However the names came about, after a period of time they became so commonly used that a lot of people didn't know the person's given name. I never knew Banjo as anything but Banjo.

Whatever his real name was, Banjo had a way of getting the better end of a deal. I recall a time when Banjo and another friend of mine, Charlie, (a nickname for Charles, I suspect,) decided to raise some chickens. The deal was they would buy 100 chicks, Charlie would furnish the feed, and Banjo would board and tend to the flock until they were big enough to be turned into fried chicken.

Whenever Charlie would inquire as to the progress of the chicks, Banjo always replied, "*Mine are doing really well, but two of yours died last night.*" I don't know how many chickens Charlie ended up with, but it didn't take too long to figure out that letting one guy keep all the chickens and make all the decisions about them might not work out so well for the other guy.

Back when our nation was first formed, the individual states decided that a federal government might be useful when it came to performing certain duties. So they all got together and wrote up a Constitution describing what those duties would be, and what the federal government was supposed to do. Then, just to be on the safe side, they threw in the Bill of Rights, ten amendments to the Constitution listing some of the things the federal government couldn't do. The tenth of those amendments states that, "***The powers not delegated to the United States by the Constitution, nor prohibited by it to the States, are reserved to the States respectively, or to the people.***"

I don't suppose anybody really thought that everybody would always agree on exactly what the Constitution empowered the federal government to do, or made sure it wouldn't do. And as a nation, we've certainly had our disagreements over the years. Even a war, at one point. And I suppose we'll continue to have disagreements as long as we exist. One of the biggest disagreements has been over **_who_** gets to decide who gets to decide.

People who like a lot of federal government think that the federal government, and the United States Supreme Court, a branch of the federal government, should get to decide. They think the Tenth Amendment doesn't amount to much. People who don't like a lot of federal government think that's a lot like letting your ex mother-in-law decide on your divorce settlement. They think the Tenth Amendment is pretty important.

If an individual state decides that a federal law is unconstitutional, a lot of people believe the Tenth Amendment gives them the authority to nullify that law. A lot of people don't believe that. The people who don't believe that often point out that some states used that argument in defense of slavery.

The people who do believe that often point out that some states used that argument to nullify the Fugitive Slave Act, a federal law which required states to return escaped slaves to their supposed owners.

Given the growth of the federal government in recent years, I suspect the interpretation of the Tenth Amendment will become increasingly important in the next few years, and in the next few elections. It would behoove us all to make an informed decision on it. As someone who places a lot of importance on the Tenth, I'd recommend reading the book, NULLIFICATION, by Thomas E. Woods, Jr., for a well reasoned history and defense of it. I'll leave it up to someone who doesn't think it is important to recommend something to read in opposition.

Like nicknames, the current interpretation of the Tenth Amendment has been around so long, we've forgotten what it used to be and why it was put in the Constitution in the first place.

Banjo said that was like putting all your chickens in one basket. Or maybe he said eggs. I'll ask Stinky next time I see him.

Keep It Simple

Frank Schuler was the County Extension Agent when I was a kid in Henry County. Besides looking after the 4-H program in the county, Frank also kept the local agricultural community informed on the latest news from Purdue University and helped people with their gardens at a time when a lot of people still depended on a garden to help feed the family.

One of my favorite stories about Mr. Schuler involved a lady that was worried about some type of bug that was eating her tomato plants. She had captured one of the offending critters, placed it in a Ball jar, and hauled it down to Frank's office.

When she handed the jar to Frank and asked his opinion on the best way to kill such a bug, he carefully and thoughtfully examined it from all angles through the jar. He then loosened the lid, dumped the bug out on the floor, and stomped on it.

A lot of times we tend to make things more complicated than they need to be.

Every April, most of us get to file our income tax returns. It's a pretty complicated system. There's close to 70,000 pages in the federal income tax code. Individuals, businesses and non-profit organizations spend about 6 billion hours and $265 billion every year figuring out, filling out and filing forms.

It's so complicated that the Internal Revenue Service spends $11 billion every year just getting it collected. It's so complicated that United States Representatives and Senators can't seem to get it right. Just recently, even the United States Secretary of the Treasury has admitted to being caught up in the confusion.

A lot of us have our taxes figured by a professional. Probably a good idea, but taking your records to 10 different tax services will most likely result in 10 different answers on the amount you owe, depending on how many of the 70,000 pages they have read.

Even the IRS itself can't avoid confusion. An IRS audit of a company in my home town a couple of years ago resulted in 3 different conclusions by three different agents. I guess you should be as careful about choosing your auditor as you are about choosing your accountant.

Of course, even if they were able to make the income tax simpler, I'm not sure they could ever make it fair. A few years ago, Willie Nelson went "On the road again", trying to raise $17 million the IRS claimed he owed in back taxes.

Now, I know Willie has made a lot of money in his life, and I know that we have to pay taxes to provide for government services. But I also know Willie uses the same roads, and receives the same police protection (although maybe a little more police attention), as a person that pays $1000.00 in income taxes, or a person that pays no income tax at all.

I simply can't imagine how the government figures any one person could owe $17 million for the same services another person is receiving for little or nothing.

If the government was really concerned about making things simple and fair, they could eliminate the income tax and the IRS. They could fund legitimate government functions through a sales tax that everybody would pay. And if they were really concerned about the poor, they could exempt food, lodging and medical care from the tax.

Of course, looking at how the government handles things, I'm not convinced they're all that interested in making things simple and fair. I think they're more interested in collecting money. Sometimes $17 million at a time.

It's just that simple.

Finding Our Way

Being raised on a farm with a few dairy cows, extended family vacations were out of the question. The cows had to be milked before we left, and milked when we got home, so the best we could hope for was the occasional day trip. Sometimes, looking out the back window of the old station wagon at an unfamiliar road, one of the kids would ask where we were, and how long it would be before we arrived at our destination. Dad's standard reply was, "We're lost, but we're making good time."

His answer was purely for entertainment purposes. He has to this day an uncanny sense of direction in both travels and life, so I've never had to worry about the final outcome of his decisions. I cannot, however, say that I have the same confidence in our government. The people at the wheel seem to be reluctant in accepting that we have made some wrong turns over the years, and they are equally reluctant to make the necessary changes.

Over the past several years, our federal government has been printing, borrowing and spending money at an alarming rate. And while the feds, using some creative book keeping, claim a debt of around $14 trillion, the U.S. Comptroller General at the Government Accountability Office puts the actual debt at $60 trillion. That amounts to over $516,000.00 of debt for every household in the United States.

A lot of politicians would have you believe that the answer is to simply ignore the debt or raise taxes to cover the debt. But we can't simply ignore this debt, and raising enough taxes to pay the debt would cost every household over $30,000.00 a year for the next 75 years. Hardly a move in the right direction, do you think?

85% of this debt is the result of entitlement programs. Federal retirement plans, Social Security and Medicare, all seemingly affordable programs when they began, now threaten to consume the income of both current and future generations. Taxpayers face the possibility of supporting many retirees longer than they were employees. Social Security, when enacted, enjoyed the luxury of 16 workers putting in for each person that was drawing out. We are fast approaching a ratio of only 2 contributors for each benefactor. Medicare was adopted with the promise that if workers would contribute 25 cents per week, they would never have to pay a medical bill after retirement. We haven't just made a wrong turn, we're completely off of the road.

Here in Indiana, our legislators decided a while back to satisfy their insatiable hunger for our money with an ever increasing property tax. When the tax bills became so big that homeowners could no longer pay them, one county placed armed guards in the assessors' office for protection against irate taxpayers. Wouldn't you think our lawmakers might suspect that a change of course might be in order? Well, some of them did, and suggested that we could add some more taxes elsewhere in order to lower property taxes, at least for awhile. But that hardly constitutes a change in direction. It's more of a "close your eyes, step on the gas, and hope no one is watching" solution.

I don't have the sense of direction that my father has, but I do know that if we are going to get this nation and state back on the right track, we are going to have to return to the values of personal responsibility that made this country great in the first place. We have to stop expecting the federal, state and local government to supply our every need from cradle to grave. Stop asking them to entertain you and your children, stop asking them to fund your retirement, and tell the politicians if they want to make a donation to the Thelonious Monk Institute of Jazz, they should make it from their own pocket.

That would be a move in the right direction.

Pay 'Em Now, and Pay 'Em Later

I run a small construction company with the help of my brother, my youngest son, and Hank, when he's not mowing his yard. And Jay when he's not in school or playing baseball. Or fishing. We try to build a couple of homes a year, sometimes more, sometimes less depending on the size and complexity of the project.

As part of the agreement, if the customers are happy with the final product, they pay us and we move on to the next project. Hopefully I have enough to pay everybody, buy my wife and grandkids something for their birthdays, and then put a little back for a rainy day.

That's how it works, and that's how it's supposed to work, I think. The homeowners know that I can't or won't come back 15 or 20 years from now and ask them to pay me again, or ask their children or grandchildren to pay me again. The job was completed and the job was paid for. Period.

Unfortunately, it doesn't always work like that when the government is involved.

Most government employees are promised a pension when they retire, just as many private sector employees are promised a pension when they retire. It's admirable that a person would plan ahead for their retirement, and if part of their pay consists of their employer contributing to and frugally managing their retirement account, they certainly are better off for it.

However, Hoosier taxpayers, like many across the country, are justifiably concerned about the ever rising cost of government, even as government is feverishly trying to justify its ever rising cost. There is seldom a day goes by that we don't hear of some ridiculous government spending program. A couple of years ago, the news was filled with the report of Indiana's state legislators' pension funds receiving a $4 to $1 match from taxpayers. As maddening as that program is, the $14 million taxpayers have contributed in the last 16 years is small potatoes compared to other pension contributions they are making.

When government promises a pension to its employees, it's actually promising that taxpayers will continue to fund that pension. The government doesn't always set the pension money aside, and even when it does, it doesn't always leave it set aside. In order to feed its insatiable appetite, government often borrows from the pension funds that taxpayers have supported, leaving a massive debt for present and future taxpayers to settle.

Across the country, taxpayers are on the hook for billions and trillions of dollars that have been borrowed from teachers and public employee retirement funds, and a lot of the taxes they are paying now, that should be applied to current services, are instead paying interest on borrowed money and repaying benefits that they or their parents have already paid.

And government doesn't help things with the generous retirement plans it offers. Some departments offer a healthy retirement to employees after only 20 years of service, and at the age of 50. Sometimes less. Here in Wayne County, some members of the sheriff's department qualify for retirement benefits after only 8 years of service. It's likely that a lot of these retirees will be drawing benefits for over 40 years. That means there is a real possibility that your great-grandchildren will be paying for the retirement of the current police force. We get a double whammy when an employee retires from one department, and then goes to work for another department, and ends up drawing a retirement from both.

Certainly government employees that provide essential services should be fairly compensated for their efforts, and that compensation should be adequate to fund a *reasonable* retirement plan. And certainly if they decide they want the government to administer that retirement plan, they certainly have that right, although in view of its past performance, I would question the wisdom of that decision.

One of the best ways to control government spending is to limit its access to the billions and trillions of dollars that should be in these funds, and let employees control their own accounts. Overall, that is the fairest plan for the taxpayers.

And their employees.

Pinned Down

I was raised in a house with Mom, Dad, and 7 brothers and sisters. That meant 140 dirty socks a week, more or less. More if we got the chance to go to town on Saturday night, less if my little brothers wore the same socks for two days, or simply traded amongst themselves. Regardless of the final tally, it was an awful pile of socks when we brought them in from the clothesline, and there was great wailing and gnashing of teeth as we each tried to sort our own socks from the basket.

Somewhere along the line, somebody came up with the idea of safety pinning the pairs of socks together. That way, if you found one of your socks, you found a pair. Of course, by the same token, if you lost one, you lost two, but I never had much use for one sock anyways.

The system worked so well that I still use it today, but occasionally even a flawless plan can be spoiled. As a teenager, I accompanied my Explorer Scout troop to Philmont Scout Ranch in New Mexico. After spending 10 days in the mountains, and upon returning to the base camp, we turned our dirty laundry over to the leaders, who in turn piled it in with the rest of the troop's laundry, and ran it through some giant washing machines. I had taken the pains to pin my socks together in pairs, and then pinned the pairs together, creating a giant, smelly ball that I would be able to quickly retrieve once the dryer was finished.

The plan fell apart when one of the leaders walked up and gave me a handful of safety pins, explaining that I had forgotten to unpin my socks, but luckily he was able to get them apart before they were placed in the washer. I spent a goodly portion of the next morning attempting to gather to me that which was mine. To this day I'm convinced that no account Stinky Wilmont has three of my blue stripe tube socks and at least one black argyle. I'm also sure that leader thought he was helping out, but it sure didn't end up that way.

Most of our elected officials seem to suffer under the same delusion. I'm sure a lot of them really believe the rules and laws they create are going to make things better. Then, when one set of rules makes a mess of things, they believe they can make some new rules to straighten out the mess the old rules caused. In reality, most of our elected officials are just like you and me, with no more insight on governing than the next person. Winning an election doesn't make them any smarter; it just gives them more power.

Here in Indiana, every so often, we go through another session of tax shuffling. Freezing property tax rates while increasing assessments, and raising sales and income taxes. We'll see a shift of certain services from the local level to the state level, while others will shift the other direction. Officials will argue among themselves about which plan is better and cheaper for the taxpayers, and each will claim some magic insight into knowing how to best spend your money when they get it.

But we've all been through it before. Big government costs a lot of money. No matter what our legislators believe or want us to believe, the new plan will cost more than the old plan. It might come from a different tax, or from a different pocket, but it's still coming from the taxpayers.

We can't make our politicians any smarter. But we can elect people that will work to limit government to its essential services, and end its ability to tax us without limit.

By doing so, we can limit the things they spend our money on, so some of those not so smart decisions don't break us.

Whatcha Gonna Do

On Valentine's Day, I bought each of my grandchildren a teddy bear. They were fairly simple teddy bears, claiming to contain no toxic chemicals or choking hazards. And they weren't very expensive, and I thought the kids might enjoy them when they came over to spend the night at Grandma and Papaw's.

When I gave the bears to them, my oldest granddaughter, Hannah, who was 4 at the time , said, "Thanks, Papaw. What does it do?" I proceeded to tell her that it was a teddy bear, and that it didn't do anything. She gave me that same look of disbelief that I get when I tell her we're out of popsicles.

I get that same look a lot when somebody asks me about the Libertarian plan for funding some of their favorite existing government programs, and I tell them Libertarians don't have any plans on funding some of their favorite existing government programs.

That's not to say that Libertarians believe that government shouldn't do anything. Libertarians believe that government should protect peoples' rights, and protect them from force and fraud. And if the government is going to collect taxes to build and maintain roads, they think that money ought to be spent building and maintaining roads. And if the government is going to collect taxes for education, then that money ought to spent on education. It's not very good at doing much more than that.

Anytime the government tries to do more than that, it ends up costing the taxpayers a lot of money. The government recently decided it was going to do something to create some jobs. It didn't do very well. It spent about $160 billion to create about 640,000 jobs, or about $250,000.00 per job. It could do better. If it really wanted to help create jobs, the best thing government could do to is to get out of the way of the private sector, and let *it* create the jobs. That's where the real jobs come from anyway, and as long as no one is being subjected to force or fraud, the government should just sit there, out of the way, and not do anything. Kind of like a teddy bear.

I get a lot of questions from people about what Libertarians would have the government do about retirement. I think one of the best things we can do is consider what the government has already done about retirement.

The government, at the federal, state, and local level, has borrowed and spent from Social Security and pension funds, leaving trillions of dollars in unfunded liabilities, and is depending on the generosity or submission of future generations of taxpayers to cover the shortfalls and make the payments when they come due. Some of those payments will fund the retirements of government employees who can draw payments for 50 years after working only 30. How much better off would current and future generations be if people looked after their own retirement, instead of expecting the government to do it for them?

Some things the government does ought to last forever. The natural rights government should protect transcends generations. The debt it incurs shouldn't.

We have a lot to do when it comes to fixing how our government operates. Some of those solutions involve getting government to do what it should do, better. And some of those solutions involve getting government to stop doing things it shouldn't.

Libertarians spend a lot of time offering up ideas on how we can make government do more of what it should do and less of what it shouldn't do.

That's what Libertarians do.

Promises and Pensions

Most of the time, whenever my old buddy
Stinky Wilmont and I got into trouble back at Millville
Grade School, we ended up down in Principal
Walter's office. And most of the time, Mr. Walters
would call us in one at a time, probably counting on
the intimidation factor to garner an apology from us.
It usually worked, and each of us ended up promising
that both of us would do better from then on.

I learned a lot about promises back at Millville.
The first thing I learned was that sometimes it's
easier to make a promise than it is to keep it. The
second thing I learned was it's hard to make a
promise for another person. Stinky didn't always
share my convictions. In fact, often times he didn't
even share my intentions.

Since my learning experience with Stinky, I've
become a little more careful about the promises I
make. I've found I'm the one that has to keep my
own promises. I know nobody else is bound to keep

mine, and unless I agree otherwise, I'm not bound to keep anyone else's.

I think every once in a while politicians run into the same situation. It's a lot easier to make a promise during a campaign than it is to make good on it after the election. Especially if delivering on a promise requires the cooperation of someone who didn't make the same promise that you made. I think the President and Congress are finding that out right now. I suppose most elected officials find that out at some time or another.

Unfortunately, that doesn't keep them from making promises, especially if they think they can get someone else to keep them. Politicians out in California have promised state employees that if they work for 30 years, they can retire at age 50 and draw 90% of their salary for the rest of their lives. Even if it's another 50 years.

Politicians in New Jersey promise, according to Governor Christie, that a state employee can retire at age 49, and qualify for $3.8 million in pension payments and health care benefits over the course of his retirement. And again, it's a lot easier for politicians to make these promises knowing that they aren't the people who will have to keep them. That wouldn't necessarily be a problem if the workers and their employer were putting the money aside to cover those retirements. But that's not how that works. According to Chris Edwards over at the Cato Institute, a recent study found that local and state public employee retirement accounts across the country are underfunded and over promised by $3.2 trillion.

That means a lot of the people who will be paying that state worker's $3.8 million retirement haven't even entered the work force yet. A lot more of them haven't even been born yet. Some of their parents haven't even been born yet.

Our federal government's official debt is over $14 trillion. According to the Congressional Budget Office, the debt, including unfunded liabilities, is closer to $60 trillion, and every time the government takes on more debt, our elected officials promise that someone will pay that debt. But not them.

As I've said many times before, Thomas Jefferson warned that, "It is incumbent on every generation to pay its own debts as it goes." Good advice, I think. And by all rights, every generation ought to keep its own promises.

Just in case the next generation decides not to.

A Little More

on

Libertarianism

and

Libertarians

(If you're interested)

Libertarianism 101...My version

While involved in a discussion of politics recently, one of the participants blamed the lack of aid to the Myanmar cyclone victims on some Libertarian characteristics of the military government there. It's a common mistake. Libertarians haven't always explained their principles all that well.

And a lot of people, through choice or misunderstanding, fail to draw a distinction between what are called large "L" Libertarians, small "L" libertarians, and anarchists. While there are similarities, there are also some differences. Anarchists are probably best described as being in opposition of all government. Small "L" libertarians are a little more accepting of a little bit of government, as long as it doesn't interfere with any individuals rights.

Large "L" Libertarians, which I consider myself, are pretty much in line with the small "L" libertarians, with a dash of pragmatism added. They generally support a constitutionally limited government, while realizing that our original Constitution fell short of protecting everyone's' rights, and might need an occasional amendment. I think they are more likely to belong to the Libertarian Party, although there are certainly a lot of small "L" members. I can personally testify that it makes for lively conventions.

One thing that Libertarians, libertarians and civilized anarchists generally agree on is the non-initiation of force. That doesn't mean you don't have the right to defend yourself, or to help others defend themselves. It simply means you don't have the right to initiate aggression against another person, or another person's property. And you don't have the right to designate another person or group to initiate that aggression on your behalf.

Just as you don't have the right to force others to support a cause you might find worthy, neither do you have the right to prevent others from supporting a cause they might find worthy. It is what sets the Libertarian Party apart from other parties, and it's one thing that prevents Myanmar and other governments around the world from ever being considered libertarian.

As simply as possible, the Libertarian Party holds these principles:

• **That all people possess certain unalienable natural rights, and that among these are rights to life, liberty, justly acquired property, and self-governance.**

• **That the only moral basis of government is the preservation and protection of unalienable natural rights.**

• **That no person or institution, public or private, has the right to initiate the use of physical force or fraud against another person, and that all people are bound, without contract, to abstain from infringing upon the natural rights of other people.**

• **That all people are entitled to choose their own lifestyles, as long as they do not forcibly impose their values on others.**

• **That the voluntary and unrestricted exchange of goods and services is fundamental to a peaceful and harmonious society.**

Somebody once said, "There may be two Libertarians somewhere that agree on everything, but I'm not one of them." I'm not either, but I think you will find that most agree that we need a smaller, less expensive and less intrusive government.

Of course, there are a lot of people who don't consider themselves to be Libertarians that will agree with that.

As I said at the outset, this is just my version, and I'm pretty sure that even if we find that other Libertarian out there that agrees with me, I'm just as sure that with just a little effort we can find something here to disagree about.

That's another thing Libertarians do.

How I Got Here

I was born in Henry County, Indiana, and raised on a small farm near Millville. I was the second of eight children. At an early age it was expected and accepted that the children would help with the farm chores. We drank milk from our own cows, ate eggs from our own chickens and bacon from our own pigs.

Outside of an occasional visit to Saffer's General Store in Mooreland or Kelly's Ranch Market in Millville, or sometimes when the Jewel Tea man stopped in, we were pretty much self-sufficient. I remember my Grandpa used to say that we were the type of people that liked to "pick up our own sticks and kill our own snakes."

That self-sufficiency that my parents and grandparents taught me stayed with me into my young adult years, and in 1974, I started my own construction business, which I still operate today. I've spent 37 years driving nails. I said I was self-sufficient, I didn't say I was smart.

This concept of looking out for yourself runs in the family. My wife Susan owns an upholstery shop and a furniture store. When she was elected Judge of the Hagerstown Court in 2003, she drew the first paycheck that either of us had seen in over 25 years. My two oldest children worked and saved and paid their own way through college, and my youngest son, who works with me now and has since he was eight years old, started a home remodeling business when he was junior in high school.

By now you are probably wondering, "Where in the world is he going with this?" To tell you the truth, I've been wondering that myself. I think the point I would try to make is how my upbringing eventually led me to the Libertarian Party. Libertarians are strong supporters of personal freedom and personal responsibility.

I was raised by Republicans, so I naturally thought that I was a Republican, and I had always believed they were the friends of small business and limited government. As long as I could run my business without much interference I was fairly happy, and besides, I could always blame any undue regulation or excessive tax on some Democrat somewhere.

That frame of mind started unraveling in the mid 1990's. The building department in Wayne county, where I have resided since 1971, for years was operated by one little man. He would drive around the county visiting with contractors, and as long as nobody made any grievous errors in judgment, and as long the customer was happy with the builder's work, he was not inclined to get involved in the private affairs of the public. I didn't like the fact that our county commissioners were wasting our tax dollars paying this man a salary and buying his gas so he could drive around all day, but as long as he mostly left us alone, I had resigned myself to put up with him.

But, as I mentioned, sometime around 1996, my Republican county council and commissioners decided that they were going to "upgrade" the Wayne County Building Department. They increased the budget tenfold, hired a woman from Cincinnati with a codebook and a tape measure, but little knowledge of construction, to run the department, and generally made life a living hell for homeowners and builders in the county. I helped to lead a group of those homeowners and builders in a quest to return some sanity to the department. The new inspector was gone within a year, but not without a lot of wailing and gnashing of teeth by a lot of citizens in the county. I've always felt that this was the series of events that started to cause me to question if the Republican Party as it existed now was going to be able to satisfy my needs.

It was quite by coincidence that during this time I happened across the coverage of a Libertarian Party convention on CNN. I had never heard of the LP before, but it only took a few minutes of listening to a speech by Presidential candidate Harry Browne for me to decide that, "Hey, these guys actually get it." Mr. Browne's views on a constitutionally limited government, and what that government's role in our lives should be, mirrored what my thoughts had been for years. I had thought that I was crazy to have these thoughts. Now, maybe I was crazy, but at least I found out that there were other people out there who were just as crazy as I was.

That exposure to the Libertarian Party started me to studying the libertarian philosophy. It is a philosophy of freedom and the responsibility that must accompany that freedom. It is based on the principles of freedom and responsibility that this country was founded on 230 years ago. And it is based on the principles that I was raised on 50 years ago.

It's about freedom. That's why I'm proud to be an American, and that's why I'm proud to be a Libertarian.